Natural-born Killers

A CHAPTER BOOK

BY LINDA CASTERLINE

children's press®

A Division of Scholastic Inc.

New York Toronto London Auckland Sydney
Mexico City New Delhi Hong Kong
Danbury, Connecticut

For my son, Aaron

"Come forth into the light of things,
Let Nature be your teacher."
—William Wordsworth

ACKNOWLEDGMENTS

The author would like to thank all those who gave their time and
knowledge to help with this book. In particular, special thanks go to
Dr. J. K. Aronson, Radcliffe Infirmary, John W. Daly, Ph.D., and
Doug Gordon, Press Secretary for Dennis Kucinich.

Library of Congress Cataloging-in-Publication Data

Casterline, L. C. (Linda C.)
    Natural-born killers : a chapter book / by L. C. Casterline.
        p. cm. – (True tales)
Includes bibliographical references.
ISBN 0-516-23725-X (lib. bdg.)   0-516-24687-9 (pbk.)
1. Poisonous animals–Juvenile literature. 2. Poisonous plants—Juvenile literature.
3. Transgenic plants–Juvenile literature.   I. Title. II. Series.

QL100.C425 2004
578.6'5–dc22

2004000426

CONTENTS

INTRODUCTION

The foxglove plant, the cobra, and certain poison frogs can all be deadly to humans. **Bacteria** called Bt can't kill people, but it can kill certain insects. Yet, the same thing that makes each of these plants and animals deadly may also help humankind.

William Withering found out that the foxglove could help people with heart trouble. Bill Haast thinks the **venom** from his deadly snakes may help cure some diseases. John Daly learned that the poison from one kind of frog could stop pain. Scientists have used bacteria to make new kinds of plants that can kill any bug that tries to eat them. Dennis Kucinich is trying to pass a law that would require labels on foods that are made with the new plants. He wants people to know what they are eating.

Read on to learn more about these natural-born killers and the people who work with them.

CHAPTER ONE

KILL OR CURE?

In 1775, Dr. William Withering saw a new patient. The man, a builder, was short of breath. His body was swollen. His heart was too weak to pump the blood around his body. William gave the man medicine made from the foxglove, a poisonous plant. The medicine would make the man's heart pump harder. Yet, if William gave him too much of it, he might die. As it turned out, William gave his patient just the right amount, and the man got better.

Dr. William Withering

The flowers of the foxglove plant

William did not always know that the foxglove plant could help people with heart disease. When William was twenty-one years old, he left home to go to college. He studied to become a doctor. After William got his degree, he looked for a job. He found one at a hospital in Stafford, England.

Helena Cooke was one of William's first patients. Helena was an artist who painted flowers and plants. William fell in love with her. He went to visit Helena and brought flowers and different kinds of plants for her

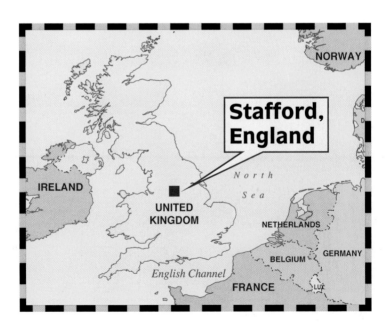

William explored the countryside around Stafford to collect plants for Helena.

to paint. He read about the plants he found so that he and Helena could talk about them. William and Helena were married in 1772.

After the wedding, William kept studying plants. He began to write a book about them. William's book was called *The Botanical Arrangement of All the Vegetables Naturally Growing in Great Britain*. The book had 836 pages and was filled with lots of new facts about plants. It was also the first book in English to use the **Linnaean** (la-NEE-an) **system**, a scientific way to group plants.

**In William Withering's time,
people often died from dropsy.**

While William was working on his book, he was offered a new job. The job would help him make more money to support his family. In 1775, William went to work at the Birmingham General Hospital.

The builder that William treated in 1775 had a disease called **dropsy**. In William's day, dropsy often caused death. The heart of a person with dropsy beats weakly. It can't keep the blood moving all around the body. ·

Instead, the blood starts to back up and leaks into the tissues. The body swells up. Finally, the person drowns as the lungs fill up with fluid.

William's study of plants had taught him about the foxglove. He knew the poisonous plant was used in a **folk remedy** for treating dropsy. Doctors didn't use it, though.

One day, William heard a story about an old woman who made a medicine from plants that could cure dropsy. Somehow, William got her recipe. He later wrote that the old woman's medicine contained "twenty or more herbs." The foxglove was one of them. William was sure it was the foxglove that helped a person with dropsy.

Throughout history, people have used herbs to treat illnesses.

Foxglove helped the builder to get better, and William used it to treat other dropsy patients. The foxglove made some of them very sick. William learned that there was a thin line between giving just enough and giving too much.

After that, William started out with a very small dose. Then he'd give a patient a little more, then a little more. As soon as the patient started to have **side effects**, William would lower the dose. It worked! The patient got better without being harmed by the poison.

William used only the leaves of the foxglove plant. At first, he boiled the leaves

William used the leaves of the foxglove plant to treat dropsy.

The front of William's book had a large hand-colored picture of a foxglove.

in water. Then he tried soaking them in hot water, like tea leaves. At last, he ground dried leaves into a powder. This made it easy to measure the doses.

In 1785, William wrote another book. He called it *An Account of the Foxglove and Some of Its Medical Uses.* It was all about using the foxglove plant to treat dropsy. William wrote about the 162 cases of dropsy that he had treated, saying that the leaves of the foxglove worked best. He also wrote down exactly how much of the ground-up leaves to put in each dose.

The scientific name of the foxglove is *Digitalis purpurea.* Because of William Withering's work, digitalis leaves were used to treat people with a weak heart until the 1970s. In a way, digitalis still is used. Today, doctors use a pure form of the active ingredients in the foxglove instead of the actual leaves. William Withering died in 1799, but his work lives on.

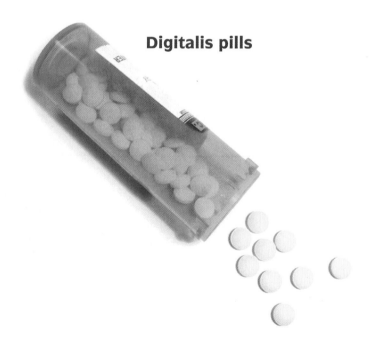

Digitalis pills

Digitalis is still being prescribed as a treatment for heart disease.

CHAPTER TWO

SNAKES IN THE GRASS

Bill Haast opened the cover of a large cage. A king cobra popped up, spreading its hood. It lunged at Bill again and again. Each time, Bill jerked out of reach. He waved his left hand to distract the cobra. Then he quickly grabbed it behind the neck with his right hand. Like other snakes, the cobra releases venom through its fangs when it bites. Cobra venom can kill. Bill Haast thinks it can also cure.

Bill Haast

A king cobra spreads its hood.

Bill waves his hand to distract a king cobra.

Bill Haast was born in New Jersey in 1910. As a child, he was fascinated by snakes. When he was twelve years old, Bill tried to catch a copperhead by the tail. It bit him, and Bill ended up in the hospital. Even this close call could not make him stay away from snakes.

In the 1920s, Bill moved to Florida. He worked for a roadside show featuring snakes. After World War II, Bill decided to open his own snake show. It wouldn't be just to entertain tourists, though. It would also be to milk the venom from poisonous snakes. Bill knew that venom could be used to make **antivenin**, a medicine used to treat snakebites. He also thought venom might help treat diseases.

In 1948, Bill opened the Miami Serpentarium, a laboratory for snake venom research. People were amazed to see Bill handle the snakes with his bare hands. Bill also milked the snakes for their venom. Holding a snake behind its head, Bill forced its fangs into the cloth covering a jar. When the snake released its venom, it ran into the jar. He sold some to doctors and hospitals, and he kept some for his own research. Bill gave himself shots of snake venom to see if the venom would keep him healthy. He says he is never sick.

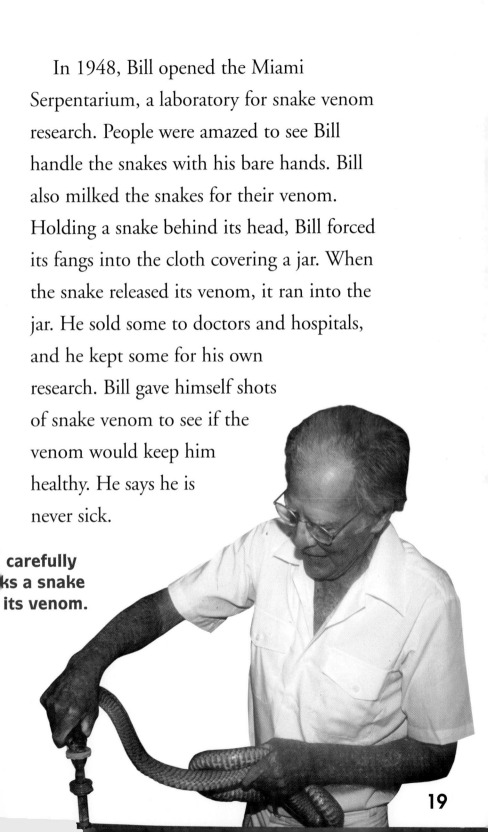

carefully
ks a snake
its venom.

19

The venom shots also helped him in another way. Over the years, Bill handled millions of snakes. He was very good at it. Still, he sometimes got bitten. In fact, by the year 2003, he'd been bitten 170 times! Two of the snakes that bit him were the blue krait and the king cobra. Although the bites of these snakes are almost always deadly, Bill lived. His own blood had become an antivenin. The shots had helped to keep him alive.

Bill thought snake venom could also be used to treat diseases. He made a medicine from snake venom called PROven. He gave it to Ben Sheppard, a doctor who had **rheumatoid arthritis** (ROO-muh-toid ar-THRYE-tiss). This condition makes a person's joints stiff

Bill poses next to a statue of a cobra.

and painful. PROven helped Ben's arthritis.

Later, Ben used PROven to treat other diseases, such as **multiple sclerosis** (MS). This disease affects the brain and spinal cord. Then Ben ran into trouble. In the United States, the Food and Drug Administration (FDA) decides whether food and drugs are safe. PROven had not been tested, so the FDA closed Ben's clinic and outlawed the sale of PROven.

In 1990, Bill opened a new Serpentarium. It has a large, open area surrounded by smooth 4.5-foot (1.37-meter) walls. There, hundreds of Bill's snakes roam free. He keeps some of the deadliest snakes in his laboratory.

Bill and his wife, Nancy, in front of the Serpentarium

Bill no longer gives shows for tourists. Now he just milks snakes and sells their venom. Bill is now in his nineties. He never stopped believing that snake venom could be used to treat some kinds of diseases. He is right.

In 1998, the Food and Drug Administration approved a drug made from the venom of the southeastern pygmy rattlesnake. The drug prevents blood from **clotting** after a heart attack. Another drug is made from the venom of the Malaysian pit viper. This one may help in treating **stroke** victims. The venom of these snakes, which are called vipers, thins the blood and stops blood clots from forming.

Cobras, kraits, and mambas have a kind of venom that affects the nerves and the brain. A drug made from the venom of the green mamba is being tested as a treatment for **Alzheimer's disease**. This disease attacks the brain. Perhaps one day the venom from Bill Haast's snakes will be used in many life-saving drugs.

The venom of the green mamba may one day help people who have Alzheimer's disease.

CHAPTER THREE

PAINKILLERS

Deep in a rain forest, John Daly was looking for poisonous frogs to study. He touched a small, brightly colored frog. Then he put his finger in his mouth. Right away, his tongue started to burn. This told him the frog was very poisonous. John's test was dangerous. It was also a sure way to find out which frogs to collect.

John Daly

The bright colors of many poisonous frogs
warn predators to stay away.

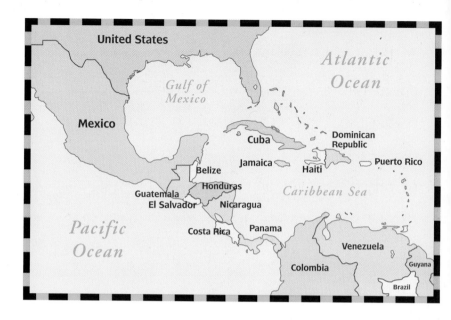

Map of Central America

John Daly is a scientist at the National
Institutes of Health in Washington, D.C. He
has been studying poison frogs since 1963.

Poison frogs are found in Central and
South America. Most poison frogs are less
than 3 inches (5 centimeters) long. They
have poison glands in their skin. When a
predator (PRED-uh-tur) bites a frog, the
poison comes out. The bad taste makes the
predator spit out the frog. The frog escapes,
and the predator learns not to bite a brightly
colored frog.

John and his coworkers have learned a lot about poison frogs. One thing John learned is that the frogs get their poison from the bugs that they eat. He found this out when he raised frogs in the laboratory. He fed them fruit flies and crickets, which have no poisons. When the caged frogs grew up, they were no longer poisonous.

John and a scientist named Charles Myers discovered the most poisonous frog in the world. It is called the golden poison-dart frog. Just one frog has enough poison in its skin to kill more than ten people.

The golden poison-dart frog's name in Latin means "terrible frog."

In 1974, John made a discovery that might one day be used to help people in pain. That year, John and Charles Myers went to Ecuador, a country in South America. They collected some phantasmal poison frogs. John drew out the poison from the frogs' skin. Back at his laboratory, he separated the poison into its many **compounds**, or parts. Then he tested them on mice. John found that one compound acted like a painkiller called **morphine** (MOR-feen), but was 200 times stronger. Later, John would name the compound *epibatidine*.

When someone is hurt, nerves send messages to the brain. The brain gets the messages, and the person feels pain. Painkillers like morphine block the messages. People who have a disease such as arthritis are often in pain for many years. Morphine can stop the pain. Over time, however, a person's body gets used to morphine, and it stops working. For the morphine to keep killing the pain, a person has to take more of it. This can cause

The phantasmal poison frog is an endangered animal.

bad side effects, including trouble breathing, addiction, and even death.

John knew epibatidine was stronger than morphine. He also thought it might have fewer side effects. To find out, he would have to do more tests. First, John needed more epibatidine. He had to learn how the atoms in the compound fit together.

In 1976, John and Charles went back to Ecuador to collect more poison from the phantasmal frogs. They found only enough frogs to get a tiny bit of epibatidine. It was not

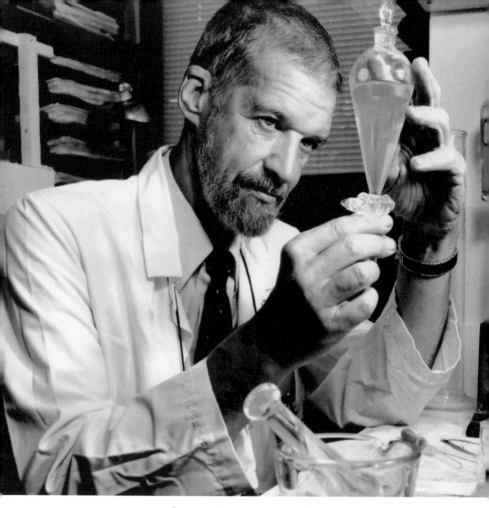

John Daly at work in his lab

enough to figure out how the compound
was put together. John could not get more
frogs, so he put the epibatidine in a freezer.
It stayed there for thirteen years.

By 1991, there were more powerful
machines to help scientists map the structure
of chemical compounds. John took the tiny

sample of epibatidine out of the freezer.
Before long, he and his coworkers knew
how the atoms of epibatidine fit together.
Many scientists tried to make **synthetic**
epibatidine. One of them was E. J. Corey of
Harvard University. He gave some to John
and his coworkers, who used it to find out
how epibatidine worked to kill pain.

They wrote about those results in 1994.
Other scientists read about it. Many
tried to make new compounds that were
like epibatidine. They wanted to get a
compound that would kill pain but would
not be poisonous.

One group of scientists worked at Abbott
Laboratories in Chicago, Illinois. They
thought epibatidine's structure looked a lot
like drugs they had made to treat a brain
disease. The scientists used these and other
compounds they made that were more like
epibatidine. They tested about 500 different
compounds on animals. A few of them

worked as well as epibatidine and were not poisonous. The one that seemed to work best was called ABT-594.

After more animal testing, ABT-594 was tested for the first time on humans. It worked well, but it still needs more years of testing to make sure it is safe.

John Daly discovered that epibatidine would kill pain. Then he learned how it was put together and how it worked. His discovery gave other scientists the idea that drugs they had made to treat one disease might be made to work for something else. Because of John's discovery, a strong new painkiller may one day take the place of morphine.

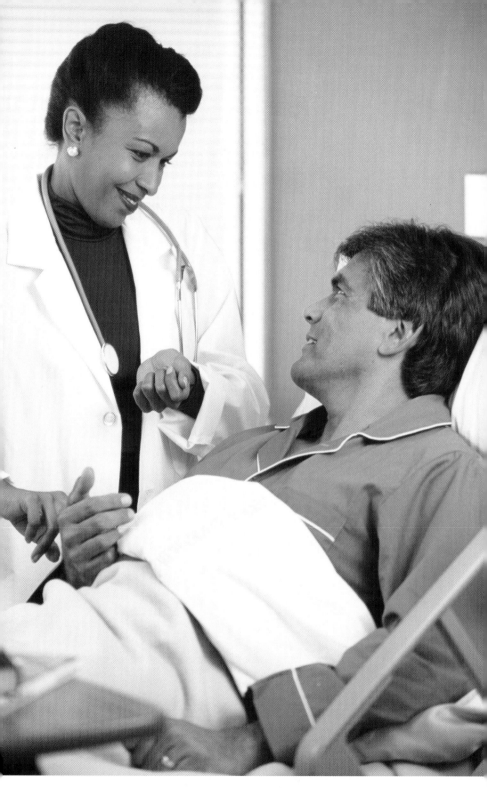

Someday, people who suffer long-lasting pain may
be able to take a strong new painkiller.

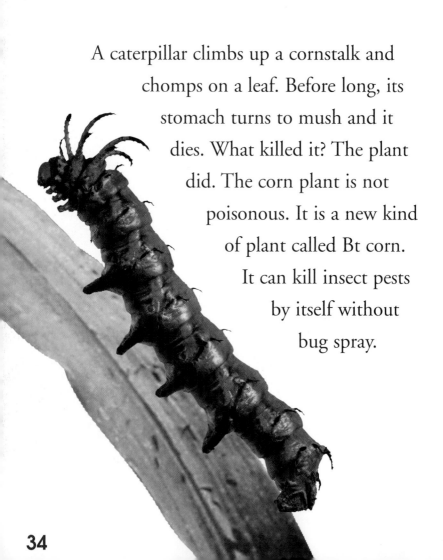

CHAPTER FOUR

KILLER GENES

A caterpillar climbs up a cornstalk and chomps on a leaf. Before long, its stomach turns to mush and it dies. What killed it? The plant did. The corn plant is not poisonous. It is a new kind of plant called Bt corn. It can kill insect pests by itself without bug spray.

In 2001, one-fourth of all corn planted in the United States was Bt corn.

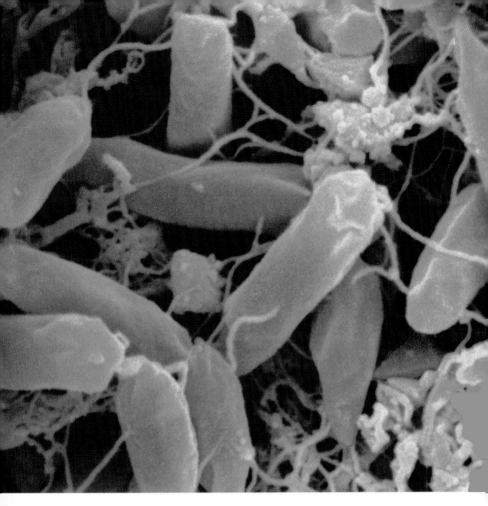

Bt bacteria kills certain kinds of insect larvae.

Bt is short for *Bacillus thuringiensis*. It belongs to a group of tiny animals that are called bacteria. When the young, or **larvae**, of some insects eat it, they die. Scientists studied Bt to find out why. They learned that there is a certain **gene** in Bt that made it kill the larvae.

All living things have genes. Genes make animals and plants who and what they are. Scientists figured out which Bt gene was the insect killer. Then they put that gene into corn and other kinds of plants. The new plants can kill bugs just like Bt can.

Many foods are made with Bt plants. Most of them are **processed foods**, such as corn chips, cereal, hot dogs, and diet drinks. Almost everyone in the United States has eaten food made with Bt plants. They just don't know it because the foods are not labeled.

Dennis Kucinich introduced a bill to label foods made with Bt crops.

Dennis Kucinich wants to change that. Dennis is a congressman from Ohio. He thinks that people have a right to know what they are eating. In May 2002, Dennis presented a **bill** in the House of Representatives. He wanted the bill to be made into law. It said that foods made with plants like Bt corn should have special labels. These labels would let people know that the foods were made with Bt plants.

If Bt foods are labeled, people can choose whether they want to buy them. Companies that sell Bt plants don't want these foods to be labeled. They say that if Bt foods are labeled, people might not buy them. The companies could be right.

In 1996, the Monsanto Company made a Bt potato that many fast food chains used to make French fries. After people found out, they did not want to buy the Bt fries. The fast food chains were worried about sales, so they stopped using Bt fries. Then, the companies that made the fries stopped buying Bt potatoes from farmers, and the farmers stopped buying Bt potato buds from Monsanto. In 2001, Monsanto stopped making Bt potatoes.

The Food and Drug Administration (FDA) says that new foods must be safety tested. However, the FDA ruled that Bt corn is not a new kind of food, so it has not been tested. The Environmental Protection Agency (EPA), which works to protect human health, says Bt corn is safe. However, the EPA has not had Bt corn tested as a food but as a **pesticide**, or bug killer.

The companies that make Bt plants say they are safe to eat. So far, that seems to be true. But some people worry that Bt plants may cause health problems that will show up many years from now.

Dennis is not only worried about food safety. Like other pesticides, Bt plants don't kill every single insect. The insects that don't die will grow up and have young of their own. These larvae will not die when they eat a Bt plant. Neither will the larvae that hatch from their eggs. After several years, most of the insect pests that eat Bt plants won't die.

Organic farmers are worried about this happening. Organic farmers do not grow Bt plants or use artificial pesticides. By itself, Bt is a natural pesticide. Organic farmers spray

This farmer grows healthy corn plants without using pesticides.

it on their plants to protect them. Once Bt stops killing insect pests, it will be harder for these farmers to protect their plants.

Many companies that make Bt plants and processed foods are trying to stop Dennis Kucinich's bill from becoming a law. However, many people in the United States want Bt foods to be labeled. They want to know what they are eating. They are working to help Dennis Kucinich get the bills made into laws. Until then, people can check the Internet for lists of foods that are made with Bt plants.

Reading labels gives you important information about the foods you eat.

GLOSSARY

Alzheimer's disease a disease that attacks the brain and causes forgetfulness

antivenin (also: **antivenom**) a medicine used to treat poisonous snakebites

bacteria one-celled animals that can only be seen with a microscope

bill the first draft of a new law

clot to change from a liquid to a solid

compound two or more ingredients that when combined form a new substance

dropsy an old word for congestive heart failure

folk remedy a kind of medicine usually made from plants and not prescribed by doctors

gene the part of a plant or animal containing a trait, or feature, that is passed on from parent to offspring

larvae the young of certain insects after hatching, such as caterpillars

Linnaean (la-NEE-an) **system** the scientific method of grouping plants

morphine (MOR-feen) a strong but habit-forming painkiller

multiple sclerosis a disease that affects the brain and spinal cord

organic a way of growing healthy plants without using pesticides

pesticide something that is used to kill insects and other pests

predator (PRED-uh-tur) an animal that hunts other animals for food

processed food food that is made from several ingredients, packaged, and ready to use or to eat

rheumatoid arthritis (ROO-muh-toid ar-THRYE-tiss) a painful disease that causes stiffness and swelling of the joints

side effect an unintended effect of taking a medicine

stroke a sudden loss of feeling, speech, and the ability to move caused by a blood clot or a broken blood vessel in the brain

synthetic artificial; not found in nature

venom a poisonous liquid used by animals such as snakes to kill or disable prey

FIND OUT MORE

Kill or Cure?

http://www.normanpublishing.com/archives/history_of_
science_book_collecting/william_withering/william_withe
ring.shtml
Read more about William Withering, his life, his books, and
his discoveries.

Snakes in the Grass

http://www.pbs.org/wnet/nature/victims/index.html
Click on The Serpent's Tooth to read about Bill Haast. Then
learn more about rattlesnakes by clicking on Rattlesnake
Roundup.

Painkillers

http://depts.washington.edu/tepacct/gertz/frog-title.htm
Learn about poison-dart frogs, look at colorful photographs,
and take a quiz to see what you remember.

Killer Genes

http://www.kucinich.us/issues/geneticallyfood.php
Read what Dennis Kucinich has to say about transgenic foods.

More Books to Read

Genetic Engineering by Penny Stoyles, David Demant, and
Peter Pentland, Smart Apple Media, 2003

Genetically Modified Foods by Nigel Hawkes, Copper Beech
Books, 2000

Poison Dart Frogs by Jennifer Owings Dewey, Boyds Mills
Press, 2001

Snake: The Essential Visual Guide to the World of Snakes by
Chris Mattison, DK Publishing, 1999

INDEX

PHOTO CREDITS

ABOUT THE AUTHOR

Linda Casterline was born in northeast Pennsylvania. She has one grown-up son, Aaron, of whom she is very proud. She has worked as a children's book editor for many years.

Casterline likes reading, looking at art, riding a bicycle, and going for long walks. She lives with her cat in Hastings-on-Hudson, New York.

Many people think that poisonous plants or animals are just plain bad. That's not true, of course. Poison and venom help plants and animals to protect themselves from their enemies.

To protect themselves, people should avoid touching, picking, or eating plants unless they know for sure that the plants are not poisonous. Most wild animals are not interested in attacking people. When an animal does attack, it's usually in self-defense. If you see a wild animal, keep a safe distance and don't do anything to scare it. It's exciting to see an untamed animal in the wild. Enjoy the wonder of it, but keep your distance.